CHELSEA LEARNS NUMBERS IN HEBREW

Chelsea Kong

Printed in 2023-2024, Made in Toronto, Canada
ISBN: 978-1-990399-68-8
Library and Archives Canada

Numbers have meanings in Hebrew.
When counting numbers 1 and 8,
there are no female sounds.
There are male sounds when counting 1-10.

Feminine numbers are used for basic counting.
Masculine numbers are used for counting
money (shekels) and other masculine objects.

They change when linked to noun's gender.
Hebrew nouns are male and female.
Most of the time female numbers
are used to count nouns.

Male numbers are used to
count nouns that are male.
Plurals use nouns or pronouns that are regular.

Tanach (Jews call as the Bible).
It has the Torah, Neviim and Ketuvim
(Prophets and Writings).

Male numbers are used to
count nouns that are male.
Plurals use nouns or pronouns that are regular.

The Christian Bible contains the above writings and the New Testament.

Jews use a Hebrew calendar.
Every year it has a different meaning when they are joined with letters of the alphabet.

In Hebrew, numbers start from 1.
Gematria is more difficult to learn.
This letters and numbers used to translate the
bible and has other rules that includes math.

Numbers 7, 8, 10 and 40 connect to the Torah.
This is not a common practice for Jews.

One in Hebrew is Achat, Echad.

1

אחד

Achat, Echad

This number has no female sound in counting
it in Hebrew, but one has the male sound.

Two in Hebrew is Shtayim/Shnayim.

שניים

Shtayim/Shnayim

It is the first number that has both a female and male sound when counting in Hebrew.

Three in Hebrew is Shelosh, Sheloshah.

3

שלושה

Shelosh,
Sheloshah

Three has both the female and
male sounds when counting numbers.

Four in Hebrew is Arbah, Arbahah.

4

ארבעה

Arbah/Arbahah

There is both female and male sounds
when counting in Hebrew.

Five in Hebrew is Chamesh, Chameeshah.

5

חמישה

Chamesh,
Chameeshah

There is both female and male sounds
when counting in Hebrew.

Six in Hebrew is Shesh, Sheeshah.

6

שישה

Shesh, Sheeshah

There is both female and male sounds
when counting in Hebrew.

Seven in Hebrew is Shvah, Sheevah.

7

שבעה

Shvah, Sheevah.

There is both female and male sounds
when counting in Hebrew.

Eight in Hebrew is Shemoni, Shemonah.

שמונה

Sh'moneh,
Shemoni,
Shemonah

There is no female sound when counting.
There is only the male sound when counting.
It is pronounced with different forms.
There are female and male sounds when writing.

Nine in Hebrew is Teshahm, Teeshah.

9

תשעה

Tesha,
Teshahm,
Teeshah.

There are female and male sounds
when counting in Hebrew.

Ten in Hebrew is Esehr, Ahsahrah.

10  עשרה

Esehr,
Ahsahrah

There are female and male sounds
when counting in Hebrew.

There are rules about numbers when they are paired together with other numbers. It takes time to learn them correctly.

-The "and" in numbers ending in 2 or 8 (22, 28, 32, 38, 42, 48, etc.) is technically correctly pronounced and written "-u-" instead of "-ve-"

Hebrew uses zero (0) after another number.
It is not used by itself.
In English, zero (0) is nothing.

אפס

Efes

Children do not use Efes when they count.
Numbers can become a challenge to learn.
It is the closest to the number zero.

Efes is aleph, fay, samech.
Efes means the absence or
lack of something in the Torah.

אפס

Efes

It is different than learning to count and Math.
Hebrew doesn't link with the Christian meaning
Example is the Jewish calendar year 5780.

Messianic Jews and Christians connect the Hebrew numbers and the Bible together yearly.

Jewish Year 5780 is 2019-2020 for Westerners. The Jewish new year starts in September or October in the Western calendar.

Let's look at numbers in the Christian bible.
Messianic Jews use the same meanings.
Each number has a different meaning.

Tanach and Torah are used with 22 letters of
the Hebrew Alphabet and they hold the secrets
to the creation and the key to God's wisdom.
It can't be used for the Christian Bible.

It means Number One, Unity, Important, First, Beginning and God is One.

Learning numbers 1-10

1

It means Number One, Unity, Important, First, Beginning and God is One.

1

א

Alef

Alef is the first letter in the alphabet.
It is strength, ox, chief, prince, leader, first.

2

Divide, difference, oppose, judge, discern, witness, conflict, blessing, abundance, building, couple, and die to yourself.

Dagesh (dot) and said as a hard sound.
It also means in or with.

2

בּ

Dagash, Beht

Beht is two in the Hebrew alphabet.
Beht is house, tent, sons/daughters (ben/bat),
to build, and division.

3

Seeds, trees, fruit, revelation, resurrection, gathering balance, pattern, counsel, witness, and strength.

3

New life, sprouting, fruitfulness, words of life,
unity, and foundation of the temple/house.

Gemel is the third letter in the Hebrew alphabet.

3

ג

Gimel

Gimel is ripen, reward, nourish, mature, recompense, benefit, foot, and camel.

4

Authority, government, rule, dominion, calendar, time, creation, kingdom, fullness, giving of the Torah (law), and Holy Spirit.

Dalet is the fourth letter in the Hebrew alphabet.

4

ד

Dalet

Dalet is door, draw out or in, knock, path, way, portal to heaven, dominion, control, bough, and branch

5

Power, strength, alertness, Torah, grace, ministry, service, gospel, fruitfulness, going forth, fast movement, anointed, prayers, and protection.

Hey is the fifth letter in the Hebrew alphabet.

5

הֵ

Hey

Being filled, prepared, and empowered to do whatever mission YHWH has given one to do. It also means mouth (the words we speak).

6

It is connection, image, man, beast, flesh, work, sacrifice, intimacy, knowledge, sacrificial love
(da'at – knowledge)

6

It also means antichrist, idol, Adam, relationship, and judgement.

Vav is the sixth letter in the Hebrew alphabet.

6

ו

Vav

It is a hook, nail, to connect, tent peg, add to, attach.

6

It also means antichrist, idol, Adam, relationship, and judgement.

7

It is rest, cessation from work, wholeness, complete, being ripe, order, stable, and holiness. The number of the Temple of Adonai's house.

Zayin is the seventh letter in the Hebrew alphabet.

7

ז

Zayin

It is plowshare, weapon, sword, to arm, to adorn, to cut, to feed, completion.

Make fat, new beginnings,
has everything, full to overflowing.

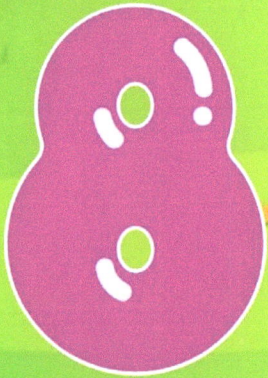

Supernatural and passes through a full cycle.
Beyond the natural time and space to
supernatural realm.

Chet is the eighth letter in the Hebrew alphabet.

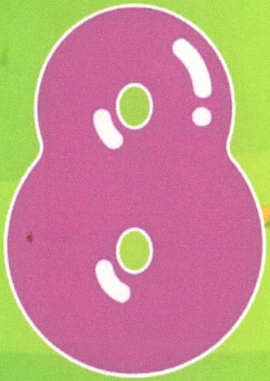

Chet

it is wall, fence, protect, new beginning, separation, sin, outside, the coming world.

Final, judgment, harvest, fruitfulness, the womb, good and evil together, concealed, truth.

Tet is the ninth letter in the Hebrew alphabet.

9

ט

Tet

It is basket, good/evil, snake, surround, knot, twist, spiral, fruitfulness, repentance, judgment.

10

Divine order, completed cycle, measure, or group
good and bad, blessing or judgment.
Complete body and kingdom.

10

10

The Bible God asks His people for one tenth of everything they own (tithe).

Yohd is the tenth letter in the Hebrew alphabet.

10

׳

Yohd

It means hand, work, worship, deeds, fist, power, congregation.

Numbers has a different meaning
in the Torah than Neviim and Ketuvim.

ו

And

Numbers can be combined together with "and."

They will have different kinds of means.

You can find meanings for 11-20 and more online.

My final words to share as a bonus for your learning.

לא

lamed, aleph

No, not, don't, didn't, doesn't, won't.

In Hebrew, Lamed or aleph is said as lo.

It's a letter in the Hebrew alphabet.

References

B'nai Mitzvah Academy
https://bnaimitzvahacademy.com/hebrew-numbers-1-10-counting-in-hebrew/
B'nai Mitzvah Academy, 2024.

Teach Me Hebrew. "Numbers."
Teach Me Hebrew, 2021.
https://www.teachmehebrew.com/numbers-in-hebrew.html

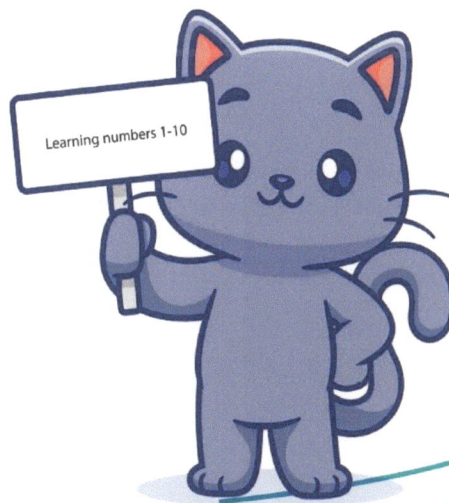

References

Innovative Language. "How to Use Hebrew Numbers for Daily Usage."
Innovative Language Learning, October 24, 2019.
https://www.hebrewpod101.com/blog/2019/10/24/hebrew-numbers/

Grace in Torah. "Hebrew numbers 1-10."
Grace in Torah, 2023.
https://graceintorah.net/2015/06/15/hebrew-numbers-1-10/

Message from the Author

I made this book to teach numbers in Hebrew and their meanings. Jews get the meaning of numbers from the Bible means. Jews learn to live their life after this pattern. For the year 2023, in Hebrew, it is 5784 based on a biblical calendar year. Jews do not follow the Gregorian calendar that we do. Every year has a different meaning based on the numbers. In Hebew, they categorize by the decade what season it is. An example is 5780-5789. This is the decade of the mouth in which anything spoken will happen, whether it is good or bad.

OTHER PRODUCTS

Knowing God

How to Hear God's Voice

New Life in Jesus

Loving Israel

God's Gifts

Meeting God

Word Power

Fruit of the Spirit

The Tabernacle

Bride for Jesus

A Life of Prayer

Live Free

Who am I in Jesus

Walk in Love

God's Favor

Man of God

Woman of God

How to Use Money

God's Wisdom

Fasting

See Jerusalem and Bethany

First Fruit Offering

Feast of Trumpets

Day of Atonement

Feast of Tabernacles

Counting the Omer

Festival of Lights

Glory, Presence, and Holy Spirit

Live in God's Presence

Pentecost

See Galilee, Nazareth, and Tiberias

Hear God Speak

Knowing Jesus

Knowing Holy Spirit

A Healthy Life and Healthy Life Work Book

Smokey the Cat

Passover Unleavened Bread

Resurrection Life

The Blessing

Revival

Chelsea Learns Hebrew

Thanksgiving

Give Thanks

Jesus Birth

Loving Jesus: Bride and Groom

Proverbs 31 Woman

OTHER PRODUCTS

ABC of People in the Bible

Colours in the Bible

Breakthroughs

Open Doors

The Seven Spirits of God

Numbers in the Bible

Aglee the Eagle

An Eagle's Life

Angels

ABC's of Faith

Devotionals

31 Day Devotional

Inspirational/Other

Chelsea's Psalms and Poems

Your Daily Meal: Chelsea's Photo Album

Puzzle Books

Biblical Puzzle Book Vol 1-5

Bible Puzzles for Young Children Book 1-3

Biblical Puzzle for Children Books 1-5

Teaching Series

How to Hear God's Voice Teaching Guide & Audio Book

Relationship with God, Jesus, Holy Spirit Guide

Knowing God, Jesus, Holy Spirit Guide & Audio Book

Flowing in the Prophetic

Teaching (Non-Sale on my website)

Purim

Passover

Resurrection

More books to come!

BOOK REVIEWS

More books on Amazon, Kobo, and Barnes and Noble, Smashwords
https://chelseak532002550.wordpress.com/

More books on Amazon, Kobo, and Barnes and Noble, Smashwords
https://www.amazon.com/author/chelseakong

Please leave a review and share with friends to help the author continue to write more books to reach more readers. Thank you so much for your support.

Review!

About
CHELSEA KONG

She is a writer, creative arts and digital media artist, skilled administration professional, and podcaster. Chelsea also served in a variety of roles, from audiovisual, photography, to assisting on the worship team, and ministry team. She also has a passion for families being united.

Chelsea has been a guest on Unity Live Radio, The Lady Tracey Show, and How to Live for Christ and is highly recommended by a Proud Christian blog. She is also a guest blogger. A few of her books have been featured in YourAuthorHub, etc. She graduated from Hotel and Restaurant Management, Digital Media Arts, Office Administration, Payroll Professional, and experience working with children. Chelsea lives in Toronto, Canada. She mainly writes children's books, stories, bridal writing, poems, lyrics for songs, words of encouragement, blessings, prayers, and jokes. The author of How to Hear the Voice of God, the Bridal Collection, Knowing God, etc. She also has her own Bible Puzzle books and other inspired products. Her podcast channel is called Chelsea K on Anchor, Spotify, and iTunes.

Please check my website to find out more:
https://chelseak532002550.wordpress.com/

www.ingramcontent.com/pod-product-compliance
Lightning Source LLC
LaVergne TN
LVHW072134070426

835513LV00003B/99